Famous & Fun Pop Christmas

11 Appealing Piano Arrangements

Carol Matz

Famous & Fun Pop Christmas, Book 1, contains popular Christmas-season favorites, many originally from movies, radio and television. All of the arrangements are playable within the first few months of piano instruction, and can be used as a supplement to any method. No eighth notes or dotted-quarter rhythms are used. The optional duet parts for teacher or parent add to the fun. Enjoy playing these well-loved Christmas favorites!

Carol Matz

Produced by
Alfred Music Publishing Co., Inc.
P.O. Box 10003
Van Nuys, CA 91410-0003
alfred.com

Printed in USA.

ISBN-10: 0-7390-8290-6
ISBN-13: 978-0-7390-8290-4

Deck the Halls

Traditional
Arranged by Carol Matz

Quickly

Deck the halls with boughs of hol - ly,

DUET PART (Student plays one octave higher)

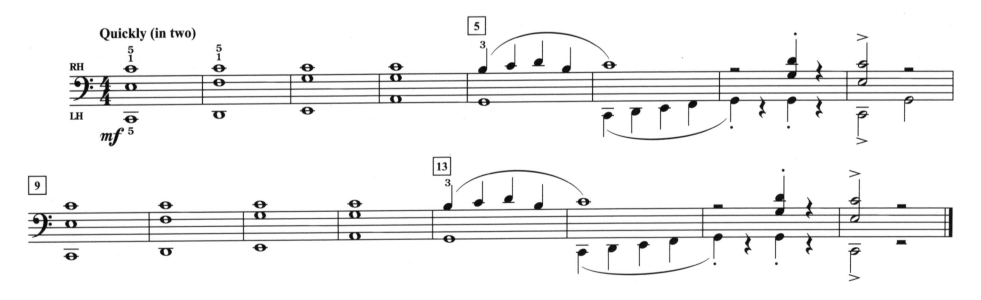

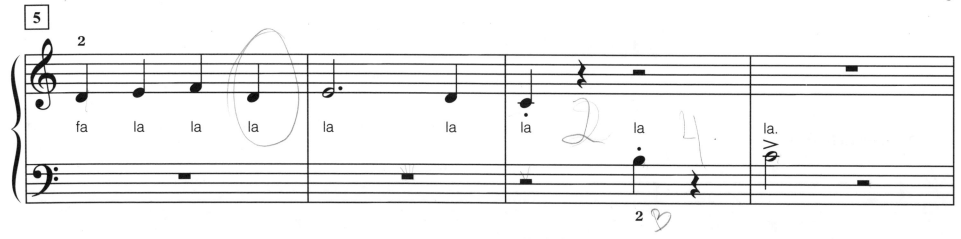

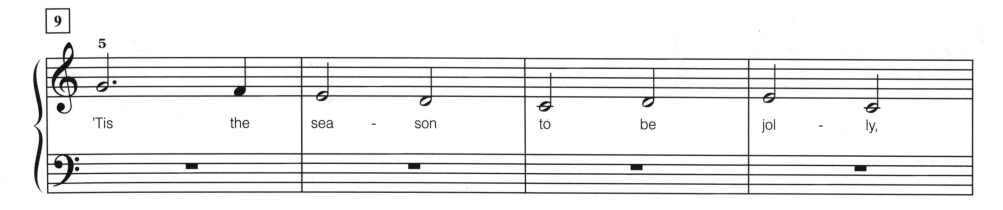

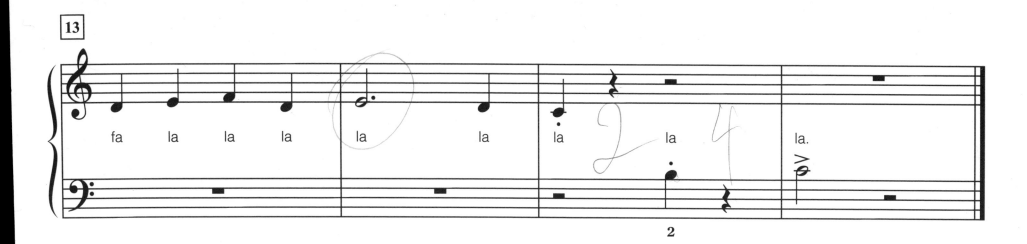

Winter Wonderland

Words by Dick Smith
Music by Felix Bernard
Arranged by Carol Matz

Moderately fast

(1-2) Sleigh bells ring,   are you lis - t'nin'?

DUET PART (Student plays one octave higher)

Moderately fast (in two)

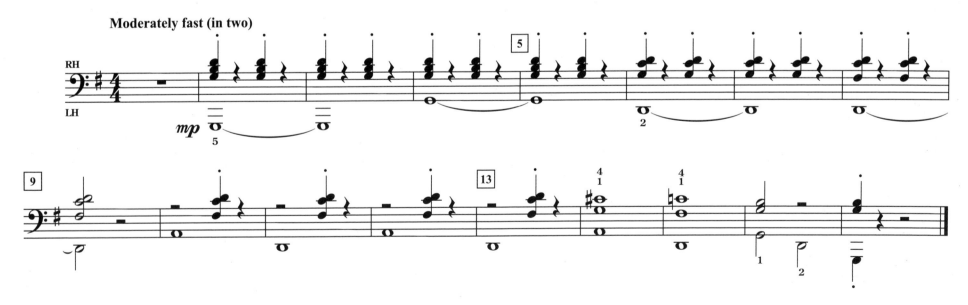

In the lane snow is glis - t'nin',

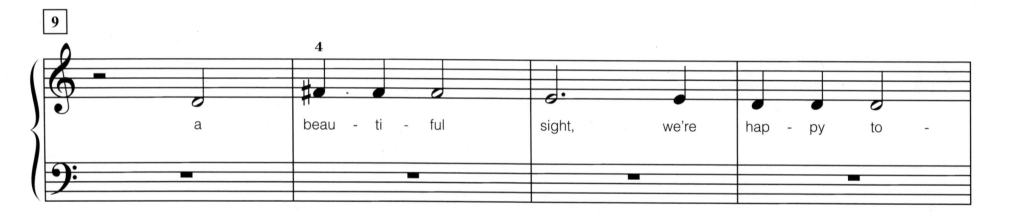

a beau - ti - ful sight, we're hap - py to -

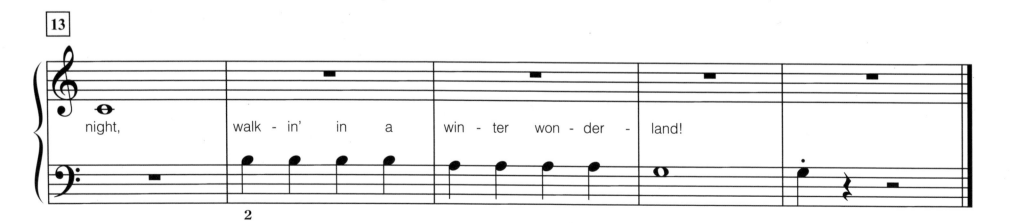

night, walk - in' in a win - ter won - der - land!

Frosty the Snowman

Words and Music by
Steve Nelson and Jack Rollins
Arranged by Carol Matz

Moderately

Fros - ty the snow - man was a
Fros - ty the snow - man is a

DUET PART (Student plays one octave higher)

Moderately (in two)

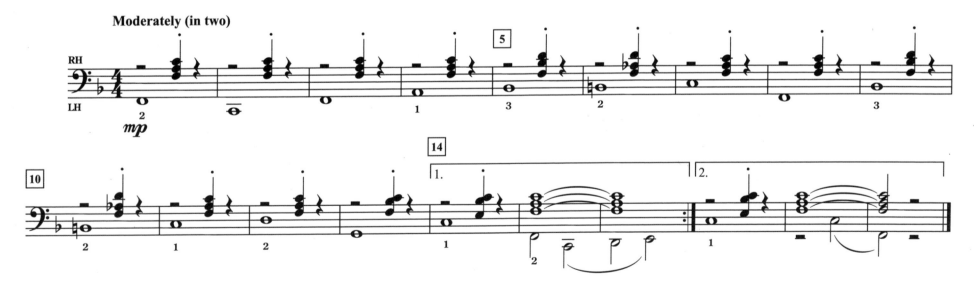

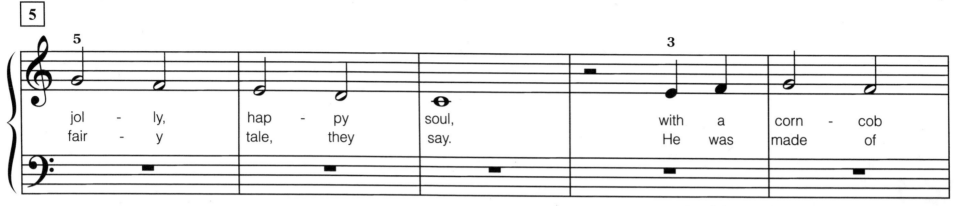

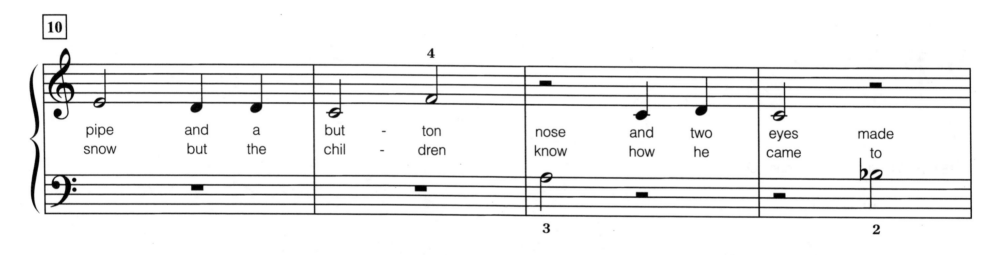

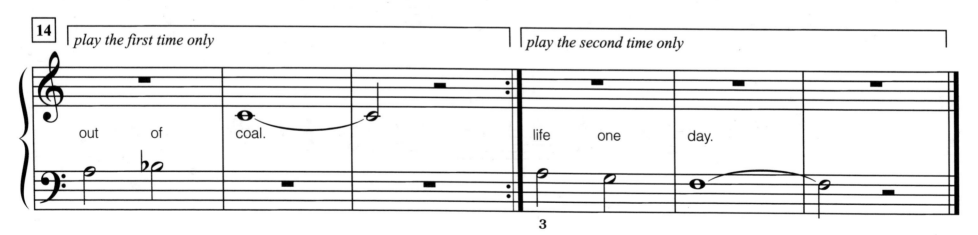

Jingle Bell Rock

Words and Music by
Joe Beal and Jim Boothe
Arranged by Carol Matz

Fast

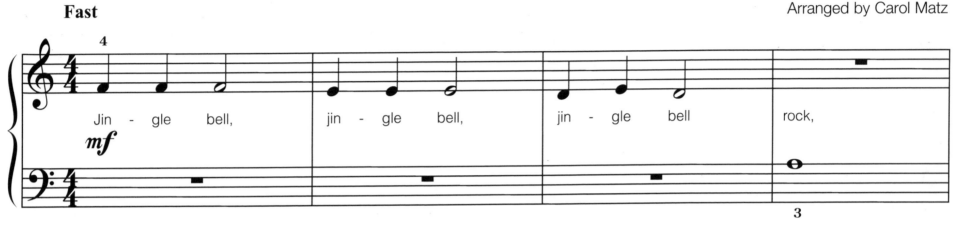

Jin - gle bell, jin - gle bell, jin - gle bell rock,

DUET PART (Student plays one octave higher)

Fast (in two)

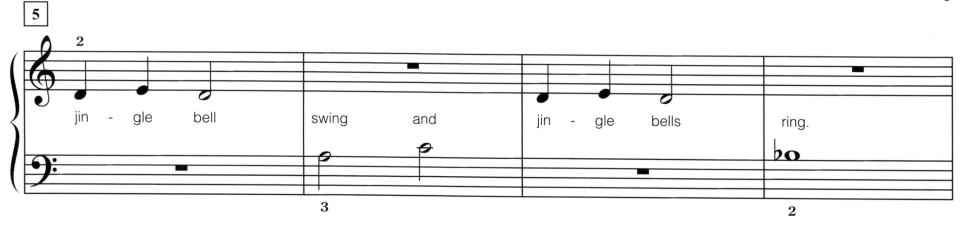

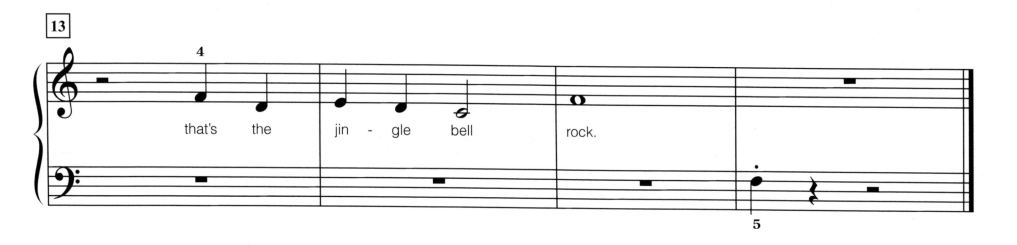

Grandma Got Run Over by a Reindeer

Words and Music by Randy Brooks
Arranged by Carol Matz

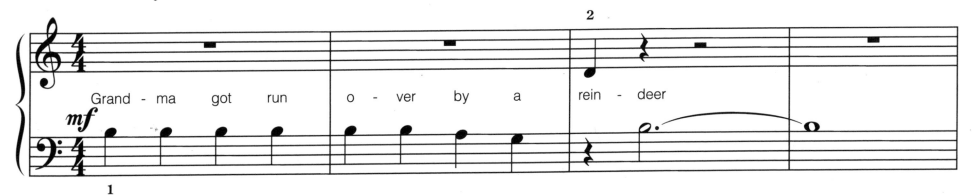

DUET PART (Student plays one octave higher)

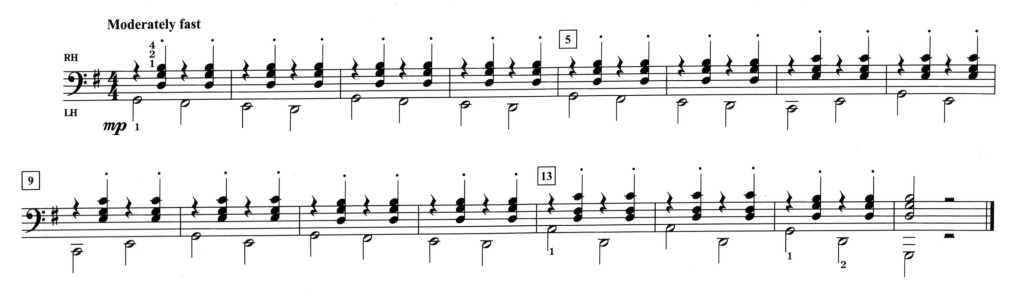

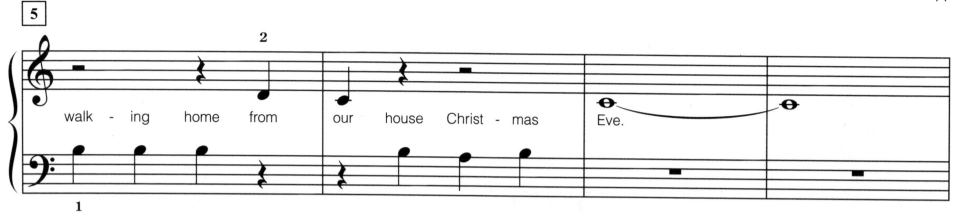

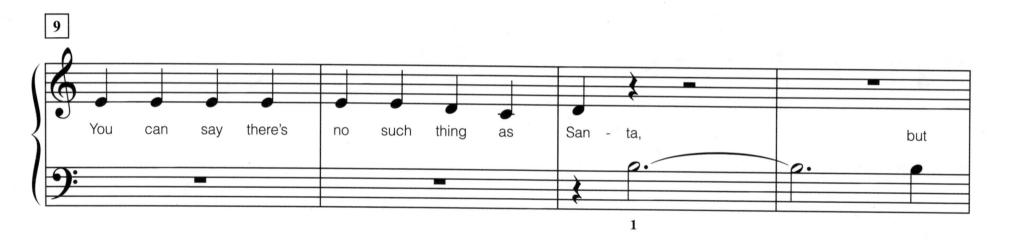

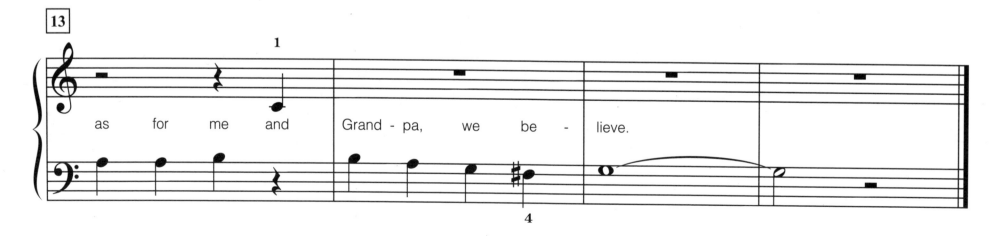

It Came Upon the Midnight Clear

Traditional Carol
Arranged by Carol Matz

Moderately

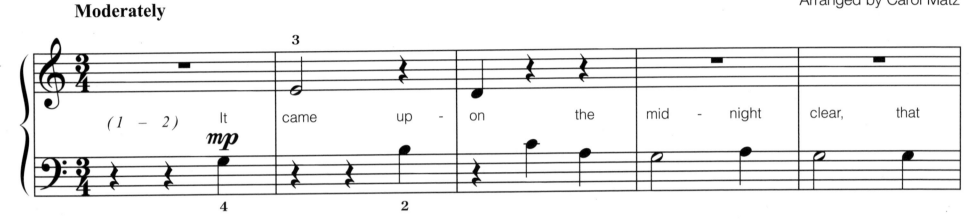

(1 – 2) It came up - on the mid - night clear, that

DUET PART (Student plays one octave higher)

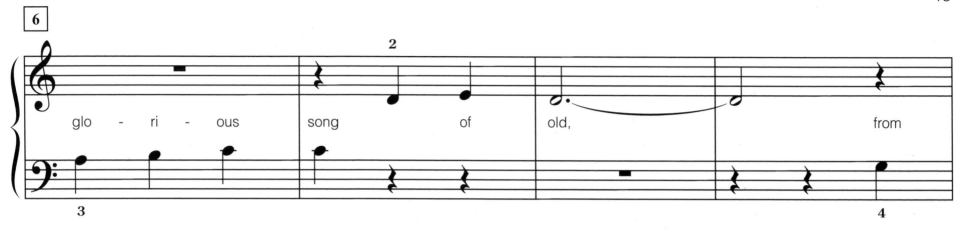

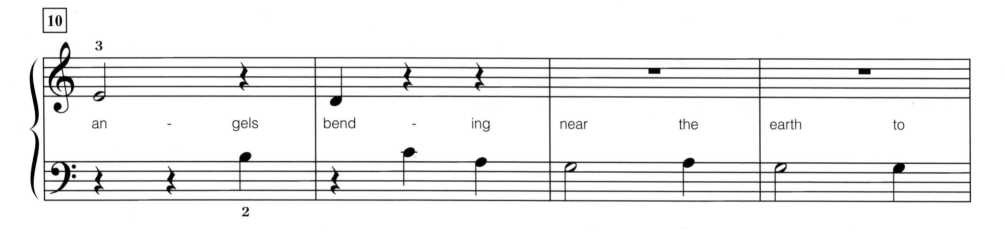

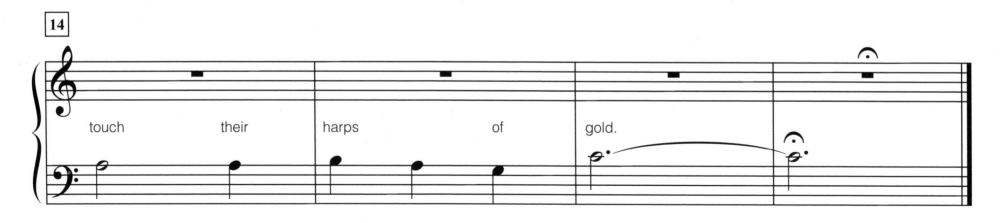

Santa Claus Is Comin' to Town

Words by Haven Gillespie
Music by J. Fred Coots
Arranged by Carol Matz

Quickly

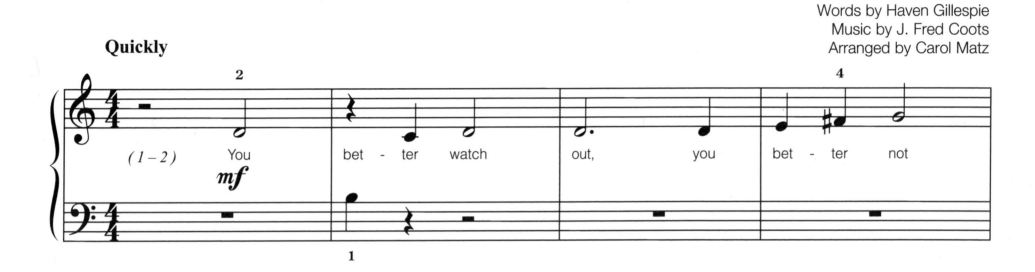

DUET PART (Student plays one octave higher)

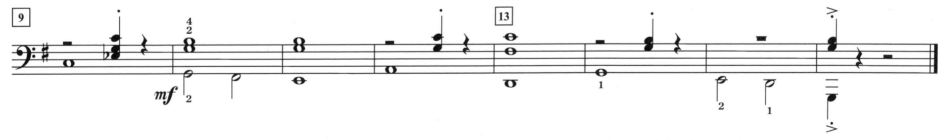

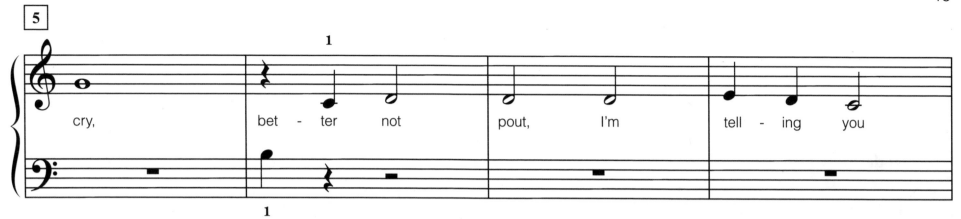

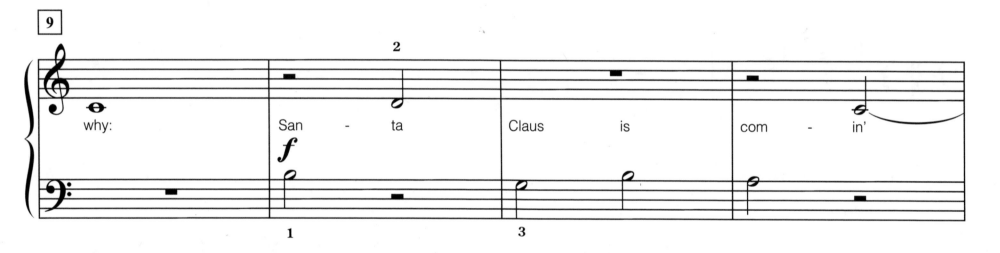

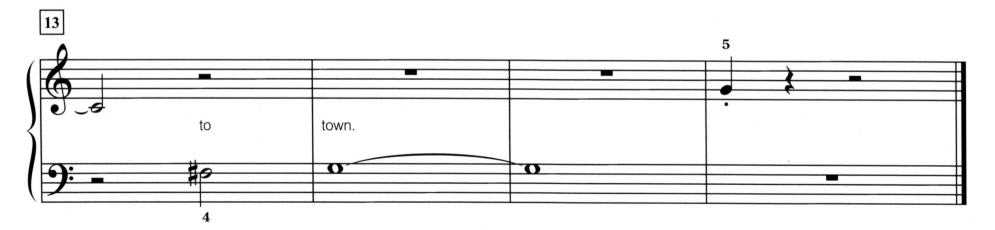

It's the Most Wonderful Time of the Year

Words and Music by
Eddie Pola and George Wyle
Arranged by Carol Matz

Moderately fast

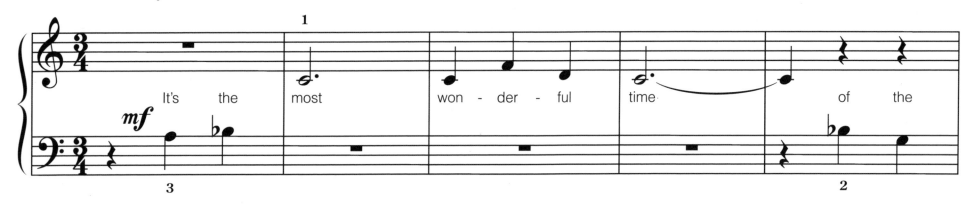

It's the most won - der - ful time of the

DUET PART (Student plays one octave higher)

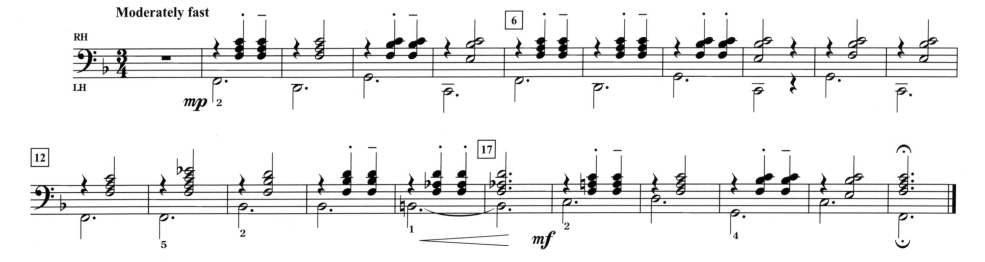

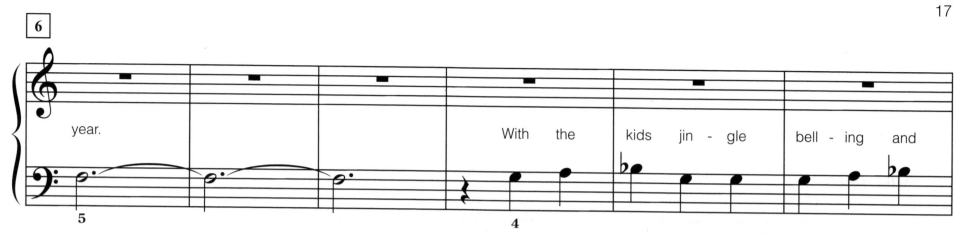

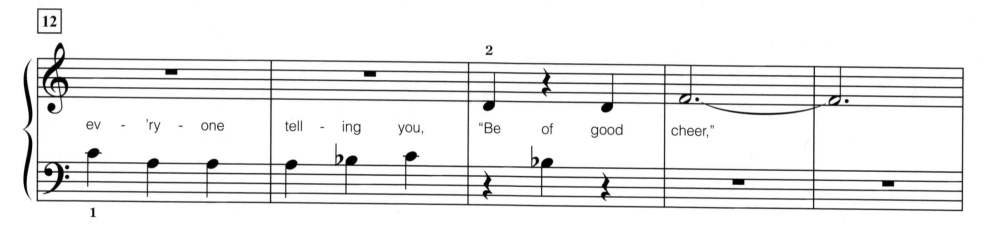

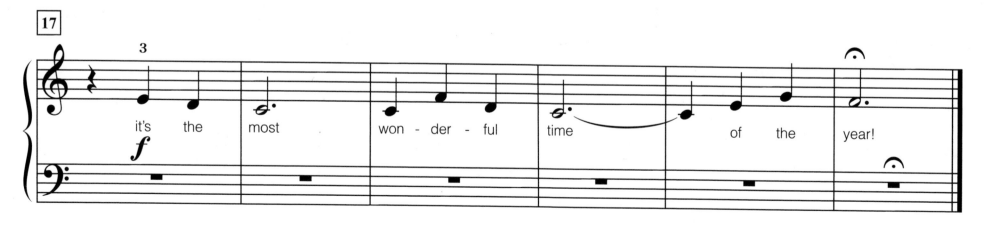

Let It Snow! Let It Snow! Let It Snow!

Words by Sammy Cahn
Music by Jule Styne
Arranged by Carol Matz

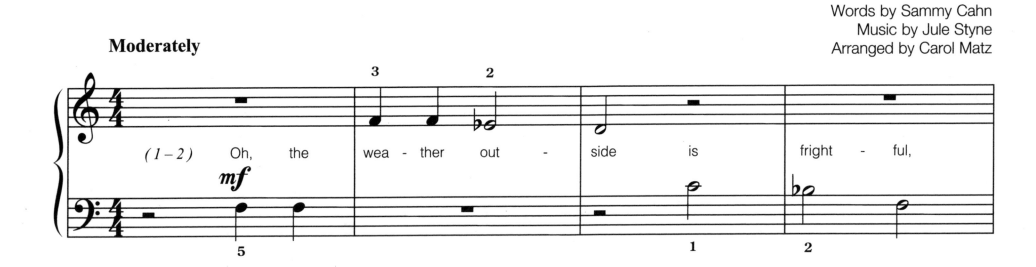

Moderately

(1–2) Oh, the wea - ther out - side is fright - ful,

DUET PART (Student plays one octave higher)

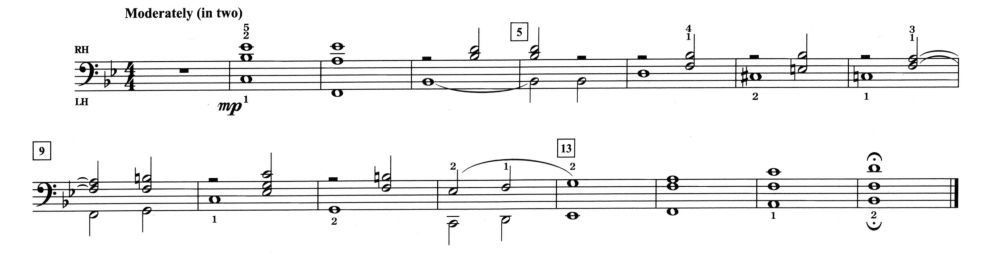

Moderately (in two)

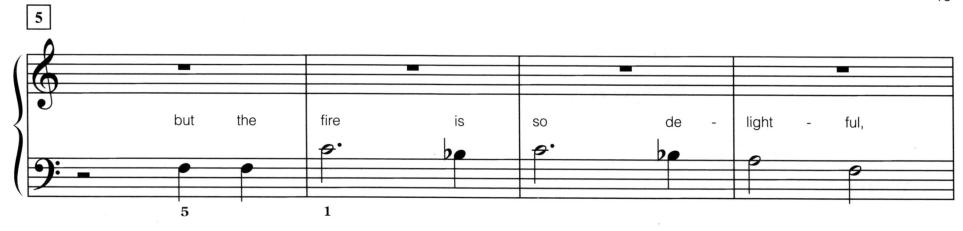

(There's No Place Like)
Home for the Holidays

Words by Al Stillman
Music by Robert Allen
Arranged by Carol Matz

Moderately

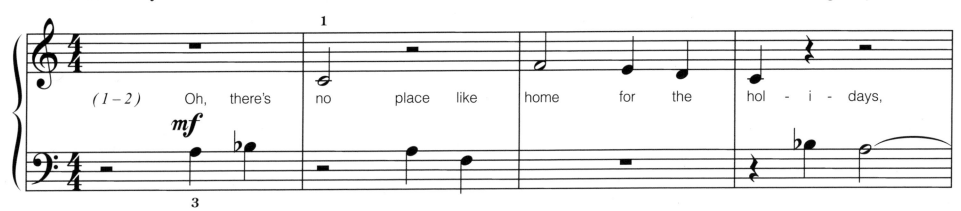

DUET PART (Student plays one octave higher)

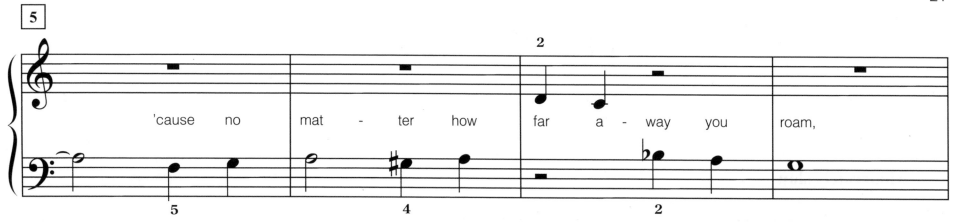

5 'cause no mat - ter how far a - way you roam,

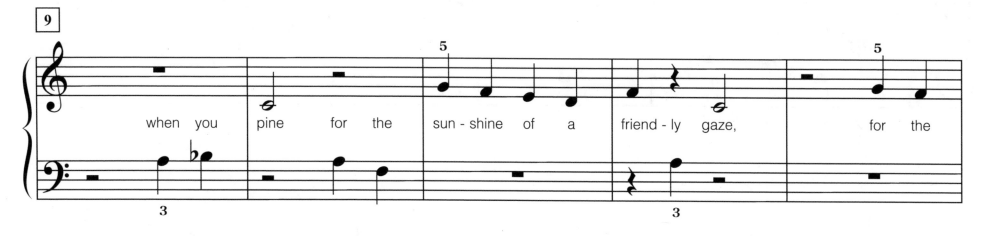

9 when you pine for the sun - shine of a friend - ly gaze, for the

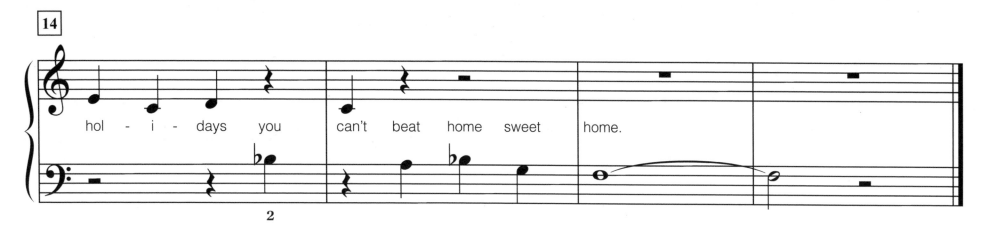

14 hol - i - days you can't beat home sweet home.

Blue Christmas

Words and Music by
Bill Hayes and Jay Johnson
Arranged by Carol Matz

Moderately slow

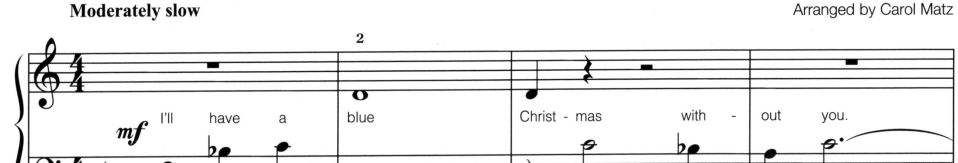

I'll have a blue Christ - mas with - out you.

DUET PART (Student plays one octave higher)

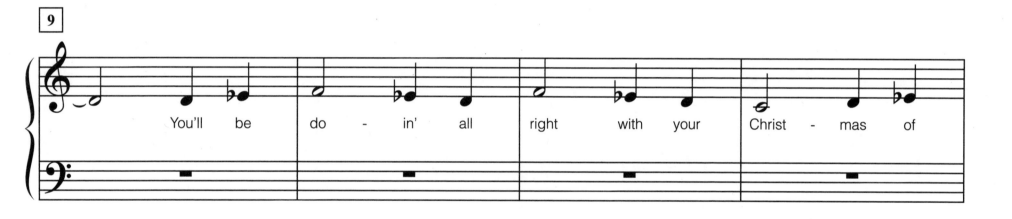

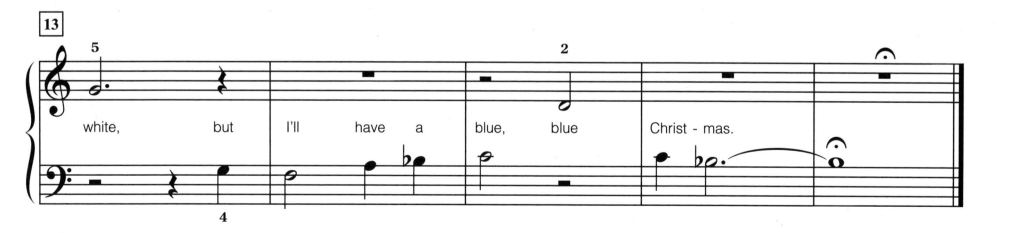